Rancho Nostalgia

Also by James Cihlar

Undoing

Metaphysical Bailout

Rancho Nostalgia

James Cihlar

Dream Horse Press
Aptos, California

Dream Horse Press
Post Office Box 2080, Aptos, California 95001-2080

Rancho Nostalgia copyright © 2013 James Cihlar
All rights reserved

No part of this book may be reprinted without the express written permission of the publisher. For permissions, contact Dream Horse Press, Post Office Box 2080, Aptos, California, 95001-2080.
editor@dreamhorsepress.com

Printed in the United States of America
Published in 2013 by Dream Horse Press

ISBN 978-1-935716-25-9

Cover artwork:

The Key
by Martín Sichetti

martinsichetti.com

For William Reichard

Rancho Nostalgia

Opening Credits

Overture

Feature

Thanks go to the editors of the following journals in which some of these poems previously appeared:

1110: "Lonely, Deeply"
American Poetry Review: "The Projectionist," "Night Song," "King Arthur and His Mob"
The Awl: "English Poem," "Murder, My Sweet," "Quality Street"
Cold Mountain Review: "Vickie Falls"
Court Green: "Light and Dark"
dislocate: "Second Banana"
Fogged Clarity: "Modern Maturity"
Forklift, Ohio: "Nostalgiarama"
Lambda Literary Review: "A Conversation with My Imaginary Daughter"
Limestone: "The Sandwich That Bites Back"
Main Street Rag: "Pretty Poison"
Mary: "Rancho Nostalgia II"
Mastodon Dentist: "Let's All Chant" (as "Laura's Models and Time's Quick Exit")
Midway Journal: "The Normal Lives of Good People"
North American Review: "The Island of Cats," "The Island of Cats II"
Paddlefish: "Johnny Guitar"
Painted Bride Quarterly: "Mr. Purvis," "Metaphysical Bailout"
Prairie Schooner: "'Til We Meet Again," "The Reality Show," "Little Miracles"
Rhino: "Epistemology Roadshow," "Rancho Nostalgia"
Smartish Pace: "Ideology Begins at Home"
The Stillwater Review: "Chairs in the Middles of Rooms"
UCity Review: "Sitting by a Fire with You, The Two of Us Planning the Future,"
    "Firmament Shutdown," "Barbra"
Washington Square Review: "Nora Prentiss"
Whole Beast Rag: "Man Proof," "The Adult Season"

Thanks to the editors of Pudding House Press for publishing my chapbook *Metaphysical Bailout*, which includes some of the poems in this book.

Special thanks to Jonis Agee, J.P. Dancing Bear, Sarah Ebner, Heid E. Erdrich, Eric Gansworth, Jennifer Harmening, Éireann Lorsung, Alice Reichard, and Brent Spencer.

James Cihlar is a fiscal year 2013 recipient of an Artist Initiative grant from the Minnesota State Arts Board. This activity is made possible by the voters of Minnesota through a grant from the Minnesota State Arts Board, thanks to a legislative appropriation by the Minnesota State Legislature; and by a grant from the National Endowment for the Arts.

ART WORKS.
arts.gov

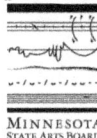

MINNESOTA
STATE ARTS BOARD

Overture

The Projectionist

Is it pathetic to see the insides outside?
Matthew Arnold thought the sea was sad,
then he realized it was him.

I don't know how the world works,
how a friend becomes a stranger,
what a murder looks like on the face,

a hurricane. Brush lightly as you pass.
Sometimes an age just ends.
A monarch dies somewhere,

an angel gets his wings.
There are 1,649 shades of gray.
All you can do is keep your pathways clear.

Life happens. Celluloid culture
becomes cellular culture.
Anita Hill's college students

didn't know who she was.
We all get ahead on someone else's pain.
Once you start rewinding,

you have to go back to the beginning.
Everything we touch becomes infected.
I won't end like that. No rosebud,

no I don't give a damn, no lovers on the beach.
Dial it back to Paul Henreid in a white dinner jacket.
It's good to feel generous.

Feature

Night Song

Merle Oberon is a vessel of light.
She has the brains to go with the diamonds.

She gives up a jillion dollars and a pretty boyfriend
for the love of music.

When we find what we can't have,
the whole body hurts, the tongue hurts,

the skull like a teapot.
It starts in the eyes.

If you want to ask something, ask it.
If you want to do something, do it.

Live like that.
My vistas are framed by pine boughs.

Waves on the lake tick like a clock.
I know what I'm entitled to have.

When I am blind, you are blind.
We are two blind people in a city full of eyes.

You take me for walks on the beach.
Stand in smoke and light in front of Carnegie Hall.

The boiled wool of the Great Plains trundles past
our too-big windows on the train.

Light me a torch, will you chum?
I trade boogie-woogie for beer and hamburger.

Music is all I have to live for.
My heart's an old wastepaper basket.

Merle's face asleep on a plane,
a child tucked into bed.

The symphony's over. You can let your hair down
and become human again.

King Arthur and His Mob

A float of femininity, Bangles Carson rides the white upright
        through the Horseshoe Cabaret, accompanied by her trio

on a violin-shaped barge pulled by two little men in bellboy uniforms.
        I've got to be where I am, and do what I do.

Her odalisque back drips off the edge of the piano,
        the black sequins slide down her thighs with her hands,

light twinkles and bubbles, and the jazz pours inside us
        like Coca Cola. I'm a black sheep who's blue.

The hoi polloi smile indulgently,
        café society laughs knowingly, and the ragamuffin

worships her up close, crabbing her act. Her float is wisdom.
        Even the Black Knight can't help but dance. During the divorce,

my father called my mother unfit, and it was like casting a spell.
        She fell into another plane of being, a woman under water

mouthing words, gesturing with her hands for help. Bangles
        stomps through the rest of the movie in a confection of tulle,

a storm of feathers, an organdy collar off of a Pierrot costume.
        Maybe I'll dig up a guy who'll give and let me keep.

Sir Sorry buys a better home for Shirley Temple. Passed around
        like a sack of potatoes by the gangsters guessing her weight,

thrown from a horse at a party, she finds safety in the underworld.
My mother's face surfacing from sleep in the hospital.

Who knows how many lives she swam through on the other side.
Bangles sings Shirley a lullaby. Thank your lucky stars

you've got a bed. You'll grow up to find it all a racket.
I propose as follows: You go to sleep.

Modern Maturity

The appeal of the slightly rancid smell of loose meat and onions,
the Pony Burger at Bronco's Drive-In.

My attempt to eke out a living
in an indifferent locale.
There must be a world beyond the world,
a door at the intersection of Saddle Creek and Leavenworth
that I haven't tried yet. Baker's Supermarket
is the place to be.

Before the Baby Boom, everyone thought
being old was cool. Looking through a movie book
I see how *Casablanca* was advertised.
The sophisticated portrayal of the problems
of two world-weary adults who smoked cigarettes
and liked old tunes. Sleek line drawings of the principals
and the caption, Have you seen it yet?

Too cheap for fast food, my dad
drove us past the fifties' leftover franchise,
its atomic architecture intact. Someday,
this would be my guilty pleasure.

As a kid I expected authority to see past appearances
and recognize talent raw. On the fourth floor of Central High
I thought I could be quiet and alone
but my work in Studio Art
would bring me attention.
The visiting artist, a weaver,
praised my selection of yarn colors.

The present tells the truth of the past. Lying
on the bunk beds in my room, my divorced mother whispered
confidences to me: What if one day the men you trusted
walked out, and suddenly,
you woke up?

Rancho Nostalgia

No one knows where I went.
From the Ace of Hearts
to the Pesos Saloon,
when they remember me
they either laugh or spit.

I could ride a man as well as a horse,
canter him up to the bar
and down a shot of whiskey
while he bucked. After I won at birdcage,
I bought a ranch

close to the border, where
the light is good. A place
to step outside of time, to grow
my hair and nails,
to let my teeth get long.

Tell the girls to wear their crinolines
or twirl their parasols.
It's hard work being beautiful,
being someone else's
pipe dream in blue denim

or a birthday dress.
I needed a break from singing,
from my face aging in the mirror, from
hate, murder, and revenge.
My rules are simple:

No one asks any questions,
and I get ten percent of everything.
I went from the Eastern Seaboard
to the old Southwest
in search of an education,

longing for one man to change me
from water to wine. I found my alchemy
the day I set foot in Chuck-a-luck.
I knew at once
everything the town would not tell me,

the way color floods the wrecked sky
over the desert. I didn't waste time
with worry. I learned with my body.
I was as smooth on the ground
as on the back of a horse.

I listened to my blood stream,
and I recognized the town's complicity
with silence. Everything was fine
until Vern came along,
nursing a broken heart for his girl

outraged and butchered by Kinch,
who spared her nothing.
Vern was always standing
in doorways. He was always using his eyes.
I wished he would go away

and come back ten years ago.
We all get taken sooner or later.
That's the bargain we make with time.
After years of steady stewardship,
we let our guard down once,

and it is enough for the whole enterprise
to crash to the floor. Let it be known
I'll go along with dying at the end,
as long as it's understood
that my death is the result of a mistake.

The Eighth Wonder of the World

I step on the natives to get to you.
I bite their heads off and spit them out.

Everyone knows I love you
But you. Take me to Manhattan.

One island is the same as another.
Put on your silk décolleté.

It's no different than a loincloth.
I'll writhe in chains for the upper crust

If it makes you happy.
You are my favorite toy.

Ideology Begins at Home

March 23, 2010, President Obama signs Health Care Reform into law.

If my father believed in time cards,
in sleeping on the sofa in his work clothes
on Sunday mornings, my mother believed in privacy,
in attending a different church every week,
where no one would recognize us,
so we could take communion
without going to confession.

My mother believed in brunch at Bishop's Buffet,
Petula Clark, Tom Jones, *Cosmopolitan*,
figural perfume bottles, the toy black cat
inside the dome of Superstition,
rearranging the furniture,
coordinating separates.

My father believed in Porter Wagoner, Conway Twitty,
Johnny Cash, making his own furniture,
Mad Magazine, the draft,
North and South Korea, the Farmer's Co-op,
having something to fall back on,
returning to his parents' farm
after the divorce, telling me
to get a teaching certificate in college
so I could get a job
with an English major.

My mother believed in Elizabeth,
the terrier she bought for all of us.
My father believed in Sport,

the mutt his best friend dumped on him,
and Sport's cropped tail with a bunion
from sitting. Neither believed
in keeping
the puppies.

Both were indifferent to LBJ and Spiro Agnew.
They both believed in Original Sin,
in throwing salt over your shoulder,
in crossing your fingers, in not crying
over spilled milk, in making your mark,
in looking beautiful, in property
and custody, in entitlement,
the New Deal,
and the Great
Society.

I believe in *The Big Lebowski*, *Family Guy*, pore strips,
the sentient power of animals,
sleeping late,
and disco
as the exhilarating soundtrack
for the last
generation
who believed,
like today's,
anything
is possible.

Sitting by a Fire with You, The Two of Us Planning the Future

On the run, we must bend our faces close together in shelter,
the long, slow tease.

A planet of women who hunt in high heels and miniskirts,
where even the most basic functions

are sexual. Walking down a long hallway, operating a beta-disintegrator,
the soldiers are flawlessly coiffed.

Getting through the day is like one long hand job.
It never gets old.

No one blinks twice at death threats followed by come-ons.
The queen wears a fanciful mask

to hide her radiation burns. Our future depends on Captain Patterson's sex-
ual magnetism.

To work is beautiful. The scientist wears a silk lab coat in red
that matches her lipstick. To betray is beautiful.

Women cannot live without men. You've got that right, baby.
We'll find a new way of being.

If we cannot change civilization, I thought we might start our own.
With you,

I will follow Zsa Zsa Gabor in a diaphanous chiffon gown
through the jungle

to hide in caverns veined with gold, planning our escape
in front of a sputtering campfire.

We have discovered the place where men are pretty and wo-
men are handsome.

The electronic televiewer is ready.
Earth, answer us.

Quality Street

The rain is a screen of lace.
Her buttons are bows.
He is bedecked in epaulets and sash.
This is a good year for females.

They can remove wooden legs
from the men. Age
is a matter of cosmetics.
Her gestures are electric.

The great battles recede
into an excuse for masquerade.
She laughs at annihilation.
It was only love for an hour.

This street is ruled by women.
The aunt is also the niece.
The haggard one is real.
Her face is wet in the rain.

Mr. Purvis

"You might die writing a five hundred page novel."

—Alice Munro

What we must know at seventy-eight. The thrill a veteran with leukemia gets
when comparing Alexander the Great's wife Roxanne

to his slutty masseuse Roxanne. Earnest Bottoms,
a country scholar's nickname for Ernie Botts, her neuter cousin.

Death is on the horizon. We can see what takes us. There's more.
Please use your own personals, my roommate wrote. Whatever

we did then, we do forever. In youth we have premonition.
In age, memory. Notions, whatnots, sundries,

on the Tenth Street Rexall Drugs billboard. I get it now.
No one is out to help us. No masters and apprentices.

Just confidence games. Henery Hawk
frying Foghorn Leghorn's foot in a pan. My dad

loved that country blowhard, along with Wile E. Coyote and the Roadrunner.
I like the TV designer in heels pounding a picture hook into the wall,

the soap actress stabbing a salad with a fork repeatedly.
We learn even the simple present tense must end, but there are clues

the world goes on: its bad habits of rerunning seasons
and eroding solids, its penchant for coups d'état.

The dying man's sexual charge out of playing Chinese checkers,
and my cat turning his head on his paralyzed body

to lick ice cream. "Sometimes we cannot satisfy each other."
Let's admit it. And not blame ourselves for where the body goes.

Murder, My Sweet

A murderer's reflection in a window.
The shadows of letters
on the accomplice's broad camelhair chest.

The dame's prehensile face,
a montage of moues,
a myriad of planes.
Her extreme upsweep,
an enflamed premotor cortex.

The villain's hooded eyes,
his underbite.
Wearing light like gilding.

The mug's aggressive plaid.
Doodles of cigarette smoke.
Angel hair on a lens.

The detective can't have sex
until he solves the mystery.

Mist creeps across the ravine.
Shadows swirl into a point of light,
whose focus widens
into a woman's scream.

Crowns on taxis,
crowns on doors.

Streetlamps made of alabaster.
A match struck on an angel's ass.
Black coffee, eggs, scotch and soda.

When we look at sex
the whole world goes silent.
It's unanswerable.

Smoke curls like a snake
in the dark.
One lamp lights a whole room.

Let's All Chant

I.
In the theater
Barbra Streisand's disco voice
careened around several half notes
before rhythmically pounding the chorus.

As Laura, a fleshy, mature Faye Dunaway
in slit skirts, slouch hats, and shawls layered
over coats ran down New York Streets alone.
She saw through the eyes of a killer
before the murder happened.

When the Michael Zager Band
began caterwauling,
Laura told the blue-eyed male model
to recline on the edge of the pool as if dead.
He never looked so good.

Not ready to absorb sex
I had no choice but to sit still
and hope no one noticed me.
Adult challenges lay ahead,
the change in direction
the color wheel took
after my parents
put me to bed at night.
A story doesn't need words
for everyone to know it.

Laura's models understood the pleasure
of giving each other topless backrubs,
delicately snorting a line on the job.
Sophistication pulls us into sex,
not the raw drop and roll,
the sticky bang bang
of our cells talking to each other.

II.
This day has taken many years
to shed the morning,
yet I need more time.
When the parking lot
hit my friend's forehead,
she lost six months.
There is enough
electricity in the brain to burn
a forty-watt light bulb.
Medical science should try
bringing up the energy,
not taking it down.

Sometimes the physical world
is against us. I hope I kept the body safe.
Coming off the exit ramp mid-fight,
my husband screamed to get my attention
before I merged into a speeding car.
I accompanied my cat
to the vet's operating room
while she drew urine from his side
with a hollow needle.

A friend is covering his body
with writing. He has had two surgeries
on his brain. I began remembering
the day after I was born. When I replace a cut
with words, it doesn't hurt. Enforced
retirement, I call it, mandatory nostalgia.
When no bare skin is left, we die.

Vickie Falls

For Vickie Benson

How quickly the chocolate syrup
and velvety soft serve
of Dairy Queen's peanut buster parfait
may turn into molten lava,
fire, and brimstone of the hell mouth,
when in the course of a busy day,
in a break between appointments,
you trip and hit your head.
Red pylons in the parking lot
rise up like Satan's sentinels
when there is so far to fall.
I also live in the Upper World
and know the traps
that mortal clay can set.
The course of fate may alter
with one rushed step
as the twist cone spirals
into the swirling vortex of death,
pulling you down from on high. Lovely
the view from up there,
horizon encircling sight's perimeter,
the fair and balanced eye
that sounds the hearts of
villagers, implements, and livestock.
Why did heaven blink?

Rushed by strangers to
the Emergency Room,

you began months of recovery.
So close you came to oblivion,
the lactate buzz of creamery
blurring into white noise,
white light, I almost cannot stop
at the site of your downfall
and order a brownie sundae
or Dilly Bar. Cursed be the ground
where Vickie fell, may white paper napkins
dance a hangman's jig across,
may sugary liquid congeal
into consecutive sixes,
may nothing grow there.

The body sometimes fails us
as we motor our zeppelin
through waves of phenomena,
a million synaptic reactions in a step,
with just one malfunction
enough to bring us to a halt.
The body sometimes saves us, too,
with its built-in ejector seat buttons,
the dime-sized impervious zones
that hold off fate. How great
the craftsmanship of our design,
how inscrutable the maker,
terrible in his grace.
Let us tumble to our knees
and bless the day when Vickie fell
and rose again.

'Til We Meet Again

En route to San Quentin, the convicted murderer
scotches his escape while docking in Honolulu
to humor his shipboard romance.
A superficial fool for love, cursed
with terminal illness, she wants
nothing more than to recline in his arms
against a limpid sky silhouetted by palm trees.

Everyone on this ship is in love.
The incorruptible Irish cop promises
the con artist with a heart of gold
they will have a long talk one day.
Dropping the French to reveal a Brooklyn
accent, she admits she is putting up
her mother in a small place in South Dakota.

Even Louise, the long-suffering maid,
loves her simpering employer, whose confidant
shoots meaningful glances at the private dick
escorting the con. Shipboard,
monumental increments cohere, making
disassembly impossible. Each move
of the pewter icon on the line from Hawaii

to California overwrites the previous, immortalizing
the most mundane deceptions. Casual observers note
simply a man and a woman in love.
How could they know that he knows she's dying
but she doesn't know he knows, meanwhile

she knows he's about to be executed
but he doesn't know she knows?

Fixed by our love of knowledge and our knowledge of love
we assume that, offscreen, Binnie Barnes's Comtess de Bresac
will reunite with Pat O'Brien's Lieutenant Steve Burke,
and Geraldine Fitzgerald's Bonny Coburn will find Freddy.
In the closing frames, two champagne glasses
spontaneously shatter
under the weight of our expectations.

The Sandwich That Bites Back

At sixteen I spun on the map outside Lincoln, Nebraska,
my sister driving the thoroughfares we had trusted Roman Hruska
and Ed Zorinsky to lay out in green fields for us. They had our needs in mind
when they legislated the six interchanges to the city, or so we thought.
We didn't know that years down the road the car would drive off the map,
not once, but over and over—so often it seemed part of the trip.

My sister gave me
Diving Into the Wreck. Back then, words were made for use,
books were made to be annotated, poems were made to gloss.
Right now I am living on the page with you, not knowing what comes next.

Two years after my mother passed, my cat of eighteen years
died on her birthday. What he knew of sustenance came from me.
When his kidneys stopped putting water into his bloodstream
he looked at me as if I had created thirst. He looked at me as if
I had created cold. I wrapped him in his blanket
and clasped him to my chest. On his last day I held my hand out
and he snapped as if to pierce the web of skin
between my thumb and forefinger. Instead I gave him my fingertip
to bite, which he did, again and again, until he tired.

You gave me
Averno and *Elegy*. I can see where I'm at in the volumes,
and I can turn the pages, but I can't change the endings.

The boss would place his take-out order with his secretary, meticulously describing
the contents of a sandwich as if its maker were a master chef.
He dictated whole grain bread and artisan cheese, savory herbs and spiced meat,
so crisp that when he took a bite the sandwich would bite back.
This summer a colleague I admired for ten years had a heart attack and died
months before he reached retirement.

I picked up *Chronic* and *Tea*. D.A. Powell asks,
if two events occur at the same time, is one a metaphor for the other?
We are the sandwich. Because this is what we get. Because the good die young.
Because middle age is full of cares. Because we are not our jobs.
Because we love the ones around us. Because we need to put it down on paper.
Because there is something better.

Johnny Guitar

I.
In the office politics of the American West
    you have to hate someone you don't know.

I'd like to say Emma burns down Vienna's saloon
    because she loves her and can't admit it,

but that's not the case. They love the same thing.
    Not the Dancing Kid, but power, success.

Each will find it her own way.
    That's why they hate each other.

II.
Emma is more man than woman.
    She makes other ranchers

feel like less than men.
    When she tortures a confession

out of an innocent boy,
    they back her up

like a church choir.
    "Young Goodman Brown"

meets fifties Western kitsch.
    After Vienna kills her,

they punch their timecards
        like workers on the clock.

III.
Everything here is as it seems.
        The abandoned mineshaft under the saloon

that Johnny Guitar and Vienna
        use to escape

is known to all. Even the Dancing Kid's hideout,
        which he reaches

by passing through a waterfall,
        is at the top of a hill, in plain sight.

Before the railroad comes to this desert,
        as in any workplace,

no one doubts the truth
        of what we don't talk about.

IV.
You'd think once the ranchers learn
        that Vienna's hired hand

is really a sharpshooter
        they'd give him some space.

Instead they set him up,
        they throw him under the bus, I mean,

they stab him in the back.
        Ignoring the muscular strength

of his neck shaft, they issue an ultimatum.
      Get out in twenty-four hours.

Just long enough for two seasoned professionals,
      Crawford and Hayden,

to ignore their childish coworkers
      and flirt like mature adults.

V.
I held up no stagecoach.
      I robbed no bank.

Why do you come here?
      I knew you would. But why?

I know, and I know you know,
      I'm innocent.

That's why I sit here in my spotless white gown,
      playing my spinet piano. It's my job.

For the last half of the movie,
      my saloon will burn on Main Street

my story heaped upon it
      with everyone's before me

who was sacrificed for greed.
      Let the others reap the benefits.

I gave up the Dancing Kid
      a long time ago. I like being by myself.

Second Banana

Never get in the way of a golden boy,
or those self-inflated grande dames,
the blowhards I used to look up to.

Kurtz's shrunken heads on sticks, a set of garden follies.
I've been an asshole too. Those who had to learn
and learn hard from me, the blowback.

Unity is the moment when living becomes history.
Orlando's head is hit twelve times. Tragedies in my purview.
Between trouble and nothing, I'd choose trouble.

Freytag's Pyramid turns on the climax, the Lord Jim moment.
But we know the epiphany will not stick. We'll forget,
and learn the same thing over again.

The dream of a train wreck outside my windows.
The house sideswiped, a scene
of Dickensian types in postures of disarray.

The Empire exists between us. In the middle
lives an organ grinder and his monkey.
Every moment is now.

Little Miracles

The luxury of summer
after graduation, no eight-track blaring Cat Stevens
up the walk. Long days stretching from the porch
to the street, with the shadow of my brother and me
in a photograph. If I could see time from above,
I would treat the days like countries on an excursion,
dallying here, resting there, inhabiting the boundaries of another
before moving on. So sweet the extant of the grid
but sweeter still the joy of putting things off,
kissing, tying a shoe, learning to tell time,
easy things, things done in a snap.

No writer is happy. Today the phone rings at eight a.m.
No one has done enough. We are all waiting for little
miracles. Get out of bed and win an award.
People talk about the real world, Kate Ronald said
in graduate school, what do they think this is,
pretend? Too small, too poor, too loopy
to know how business works. Manipulated
bastards calling the shots, untethered
from common sense.

Walking up the long, cracked cement in senior year
I opened the screen door to my mother on her knees
soaping the wall-to-wall, a half-eaten sandwich in her hands,
Bobby Goldsboro in the air. Like her, I hoped
for a sudden savior, a happy surprise, I mean,
a summer job at the end of summer, college acceptance
on incomplete applications. I've worked for men who counted on

last-minute miracles, novitiates to zeitgeist,
incapable of strategic planning,
the discipline of months.
On the news a gaggle of cops
kicks a downed man. The professor explains
because they uphold the law
anything they do is right.

My older sister and I exhibited wacky,
risky behaviors. Kicked in the seat of the pants out of the house,
we slept in the park overnight. With Morgan Kidder,
I smoked pot in my bedroom, my family in the next room
watching *Three's Company*. My sister sheared her hair off.
When I needed a place to live,
I knocked on doors.
When I was running out of money,
I bought food for next week.

In the office, I had the boss from another planet,
a twenty-first century determinist.
Desperate, I began to speak in clichés.
You can't be all things to all people.
No good deed goes unpunished.
If you lie down with dogs you get up with fleas.
Don't pee on my leg and tell me it's raining.
My life is an open book, I said.
He returned fire with a flaccid
it is what it is, you know what I mean,
and I can't be bothered.

My younger sister never went to college.
At thirteen she taught herself how to drive a car.
One day she sat behind the steering wheel and turned the key.

Beyond the Rocks

Entropy is our parlor.
Famous people touched these objects.

Because Narcissus looked into this fountain,
it is my home. Meaning comes from repetition.

The work of the day commences,
as they delve into the mysteries of the past.

The old husband dies
in the embrace of his betrayers,

the young lovers. The script
compels the enemies to hold hands.

Hassan Ben Ali, chief of a band of desert marauders,
respects no law—human or divine.

We've discovered the ruins
where liars were chained to pillars in a sandstorm.

Today, I'm performing in a pageant
that pays homage to the god of murder.

Man Proof

Color is in the air between us. Call it Spiritus Mundi
or the collective unconscious, it is the teal and salmon
of the upholstered headboard, the ivory of the sheers
around the four-poster bed, the Windsor blue
and Persian cream of my dressing gown's floral print.

I've been neither one thing nor another. The world you see
is not the world I live in. No silver balloon floating on a string
behind the white stripes of Venetian blinds.
For me it is primary red, an ache of the in-step,
Franchot Tone sweating under the lights.

I'm nothing but a nothing. Let's mock the barbarians in the ring.
No matter if they look like John Garfield and William Holden,
William Butler Yeats and C.G. Jung. Maybe someday I'll see my face up there.
Forgiveness is okay. I want the story to end before it becomes a story.
Hello, Mother. I'll wager I look great in a blonde wig.

You talk and I'll listen. Franchot Tone folds like a bad hand.
Tell the story backward and the balloon recedes behind a door.
My memory is your memory, my dreams are your dreams.
If I am standing on a cliff, you are on the other side. Goodbye, Mother.
It was a good fight, and the better man won. Anyone got a ducat?

The Reality Show

Nervous and too public, Tillie smothers Emily with anxious love,
        shuffling her off to the convalescent home for teens

at the bidding of the zeitgeist. I cannot become cold
        in front of the blackboard, my shins covered in sequins.

When Maxine's nameless aunt brought shame to the family
        through illegitimate pregnancy, the villagers pillaged the farm,

murdering pigs, chickens, and cows. More of the economic pie
        for me, the rapist said afterward. It's not the doctors,

and the lawyers, and the factory bosses themselves.
        It's what floats in the air that rules us, our mad attempts

to figure out the puzzle, to guess our positions on the board
        and jump ahead. In spite of the Cold War, Emily becomes

a gifted actress. Maxine counsels veterans in sunny California.
        Pointing my finger at individuals while I address the group,

I speak the language of people living on subtlety.
        It is a long road to moxie. Clad in a coat of eyes,

we bear the headache of injustice, our every movement
        part of the record, writing stories backward to make sense.

The Face Behind the Mask

When I met him on the pier at night,
streetlights' reflections wriggling
on the embankment
like some crazy static,

I told him, a mangled face,
that ain't nothing. I smiled at him
like we was on a date, even though,
slinking along in a black fedora

and his collar up, he was in the flesh
the monster from under the bed.
I knew what he was thinking
before we met. I was back there

flipping a coin to see if I'd stop him
or if I wouldn't. Oh, it was just some sporting interest.
Heads he jumps and tails he doesn't.
Heads I saves him and tails I doesn't.

My name is Dinky, what's yours?
Janos, he told me, Janos Szabo.
What do you get out of being dead,
I said. Laying in a grave ain't my idea of life.

We was meant for each other
like his face was meant for that mask.
We wanted the same things.
A good hot and cold water hotel,

four square meals, music. I took care of him,
and he took care of me. I didn't want to squeal
on him and Helen, trading in a life of crime
for a house with green shutters,

but Jeff and the mob held my feet to the fire.
Even then, shot and thrown from a car,
last thing I did before dying was call and warn him,
Don't turn on the radio, beware of what you love.

It can kill you. Like I said on the pier,
I'm looking at you, and I'm talking to you.
Hey, you're pretty lucky
to find a guy like me.

London in the Dark

Nothing is more comfortable than a mystery.
>>He is never more at home than tied up in a trunk,
>>>>he is never more at rest than giving chase.

The detective's tool is disguise. The villain's tool is aphorism.
>>I will show up at my desk and wait every day until I die.
>>>>Cars slip through the city's empty streets at night.

These shadows are as thick as history.
>>England will need years to wipe them off,
>>>>Coventry, Birmingham, Bath. The villain's crime is killing time.

This is the decade of my greatest potential.
>>An ultimatum in gift wrap. An abacus of skulls.
>>>>I will start over. A bookcase turns into a door.

Sherlock Holmes turns into a wharf rat. He dances swing,
>>he jives to boogie woogie. Miss Eberli's flat
>>>>is a rectangle of light in the city's dark grid.

These windows are unbreakable.
>>I was looking for something ingenious,
>>>>and instead I found something ingenuous.

The apparatus drips at regular intervals, leaving a luminous path.
>>I will follow it to the speedboat docked in the Thames,
>>>>to the mouth of the workday. An innocent man

under a spotlight, the kidnapped inventor.
>>Holmes lives another hundred years in the rain.
>>>>What would we do without weather?

Epistemology Roadshow

Wind busies the bare branches.
And always the birds diving the feeder.

Phrases from an antiques program:
folly, ephemera, provenance.

The author of *Don't Sweat the Small Stuff*
died unexpectedly at age forty-five.

China sleeps in my basement.
I write without seeing.

Querulous Paul Lynde says goodbye
to wife Imogene Coca

in *Under the Yum Yum Tree*,
"See you at lunch. I can't wait."

Keep reaching into the past
to grab something new.

Here is the spine of the poem:
I will find worth there.

I will hold worry
like a rocket.

I'll kick it in the sand.
I will lay it down.

I will bring my case
to the table.

I will ready myself
for an appraisal.

Chairs in the Middles of Rooms

A bathrobe, a table, a lamp,
a bottle of gin.

The interior of every late show.

I wanted old things when I was young,
my birthright.

My mother bought us
candy and pop
for our silence,

hours at the bar
while the Hamm's sign's waves crashed
with the regularity

of throwing back beers.

Staying overnight
with a fifth-grade classmate
in a row house on Thirteenth,

I couldn't sleep.
I pointed my face out the window
to the concrete blocks.

Said goodbye in the morning
on an elaborately turned wood staircase.

My father and stepmother
sold an antique pitcher and washbasin
from our deserted farmhouse attic.

Dreams in the movies
always scared me as a kid.
Spider webs and cracked glass.

When I grew up
I wanted to be a little old man.

Driving at night,
the dashboard
lit my father's face from below.

A Parkour court in Leicester
will reduce antisocial behavior
among young men.

The flabby third acts of American lives,
a cotillion of bloat, poor motility,
the easy. "A bore is starred,"

the *Village Voice* wrote of Streisand's
remake that I watched on the plane here,
her four-octave range squandered.

With the collapse of Goldtrail Holidays,
the CAA wonders how to bring
stranded holidaymakers home.

Bjork bails out Iceland
whose bust wiped out Nottingham.
Not all chronology is decadence and science.

"Load every rift . . . with ore," Keats told Shelley.
Yarn becomes a bow in a flash of hands,
butterfly bushes grow wild along the tube,

and swallows spiral and bank like hive mind.
No other physical challenge is as difficult
as holding a life in my ears.

A BBC Three program tells us that chronology
is more than the immaculate degeneration of our cells.
Depth of field is a corridor of stars,

and Clouds of Magellan shimmer
like Dame Edna's rhinestones, an excrescence
of Easter grass, excelsior, a cabinet of Swarovski

crystals at Harrods, the surfeit of light that absorbs us
as we walk across the ocean floor
from the island to the mainland at low tide.

Nostalgiarama

So much elegant suffering.
The mute girl in *The Spiral Staircase*.
The shapely maid who says to her boyfriend,
oh darling, I'm so unhappy.

How I wanted to say that to someone.
When I got the chance, he tired of hearing it.
I measured time by how far away I could live.

A dog-eared paperback, Joanna Russ's *The Female Man*.
What if the Great Depression never ended?
We'd all be wearing fedoras and zoot suits
snoods and rats, spending ration stamps.

My mom used to empty out the attic.
My dad took everything in the divorce.
All the stuff I've saved. Sheer drapes and cut glass.
Everything from the decree.
I asked for the quilt back. It was in rags.

We wish not to stop the passage of time,
but the ending of eras. My dad used to say,
children should be seen and not heard,
quoting Queen Victoria in a Midwestern bowling alley.

A friend bought two copies of Madonna's *Sex*,
one to read, one to save.
Living in one place long enough,
scary monsters in the basement

join us in the living room,
their mojo switched off.
We've got to drop it. This is all we get,
living through and not after
what happens to the body.

Undercurrent

I.
It is not so hard to believe
that one's husband
has murdered his brother

once you have time
to get used to the notion,
Jayne Meadows

tells Katharine Hepburn
in Vincente Minnelli's
dizzying film noir.

II.
Her husband,
with his fine eye
for the details of women's clothes,

has transformed Hepburn's
sporty tomboy
from confident screwball

to stylish, mature victim.
As her silhouette
has sharpened

her confidence has eroded.
Even her crisp diction
has softened with confusion.

III.
How we want to believe
that experiences
contain lessons,

a past event
dictates the present,
which encrypts the future.

IV.
Her husband,
a munitions magnate,
murdered a Jewish refugee

in his employ,
and took credit for the invention
that defeated the Nazis.

The movie asks us to believe
she loves her husband's brother instead,
even though she has never met him.

V.
The husband
is played by glamorous
Robert Taylor,

while the brother
is played by brooding
Robert Mitchum.

Everything we know about the movies
tells us her husband's sin
will be forgiven.

Only later do we wonder
if the brother is as guilty as the husband
for keeping the secret.

VI.
A life without fear,
her husband vows.
He has feared his brother

for knowing the truth,
but has shed his weakness.
His fear has transformed

into anger. Either
he must tell his wife
or kill her.

When he offers her
a cup of coffee
at breakfast,

the camera looks at her
as if through water,
the manifold planes

of her raw-boned face
blurred, a woman
on the verge of drowning.

VII.
What it is like
to hear other people
talking about you,

and to hear it
in the presence of others:
The bottom of your stomach

falling out.
In the hotel lobby
the wife and husband overhear

two acquaintances
mocking her naiveté.
On the elevator ride up

Hepburn fumes in silence.
When her husband
humors her, she lashes out.

She opens our eyes
to what we had seen
but not recognized.

This is the inheritance
from our parents, the movies they watched,
the mid-century formula

for adulthood, a world
whose largeness and corruption
is beyond our grasp,

where motivation is visible only
to those whose sophistication
makes them worthy.

VIII.
The condoned habit
of scapegoating
we have to correct,

the ideas we breathe
come out through our hands,
are left in our paths,

and mark our walls.
The modes of a century
configure into the masks

we assume in the course
of a day, as needed.
At the end of the movie,

the husband is dead
and the wife
is with the brother.

We believe in the power of stories,
of the beginning's compulsion
to evolve into the middle

and the middle's need
to metamorphose into the end.
In our fierce determinism

we forget the apocryphal insertion,
the inherent appeal of the alternative spiral,
incendiary in the helix of the DNA,

able to lead to new roles,
and to scrap the past. Beginning,
middle, end.

Barbra

First her clothes   Black full-length dress slit up to the thigh
Green emerald jacket belted at the waist   Then the naked man in
the locker room   Then the moue she pulls   when Ryan O'Neal
asks if she could live with his body on her head   Summer of
'78   Jimmy Carter   Open space between junior and senior
year   Varnish of sweat on skin   Chill in the air   Busboys at
Spaghetti Works   The charge of asking him to a poetry reading
Exchanging poems   Interstitial   He said that was a word   Lunch
at King Fong's   Slurping his food   Wild hair against gaunt cheeks
Austere is a word that sounds like its meaning   Hadassah Bargain
Box near his apartment on Dodge   Walking and arguing ideas
Coffee with cream sky above the incinerator on the north side of
downtown   When we reached agreement I turned and walked
away   My sister Rita took me to *The Main Event*   Westroads
Cinema   Kathy Bohi in a chenille jacket in the lobby   The turn
of her calf in Geometry   Barbra plays a bankrupt executive whose
last asset is a washed up fighter   Her boyfriend told her she had
a great ass   As the producer he featured it in many scenes   In
interviews she said she never liked her looks although now knows
she was beautiful in her thirties   Wearing a shorty bathrobe she
vacuums her pink apartment   She smokes a cigarette like a man
when she catches Kid Natural in a lie   She mispronounces Brent
Musburger's name and hijacks his sports show over the credits
Most audiences were annoyed   At the end her voice breaks
free   Soaring synthesizers   Multiple key changes   A rise in
octave   An impossibly long note   Engine of music   A machine
cranked faster and faster   This was my future   Paul Jabara's
song winning an Oscar   Jimmy Carter in office   Harvey Milk
elected in San Francisco   Sunsets at Elmwood Park   Home of

Warren Buffet   Rita's new Famolare shoes in the mud   Oaky
wine   Heavy sediment   Muenster cheese from Hickory Farms
When I grow up I don't want to be a stooge for daytime TV
Judge Judy outstretches her arms like Evita   Her Botoxed face is
smooth   Beastly Expressions a category on *Jeopardy*   A sellout
A company man   Today the sun was directly above the equator
The day was as long as the night   Jimmy Carter calls resistance
to health care reform racism   This is what it looks like people
Your friends and neighbors   The pedophile in the cubicle down
Don't insult our intelligence   Call it what it is   How to get out
of this   When I graduated I shopped at the Goodwill for my
future life   An iridescent saucer   A pink swan TV lamp   Pearl
Methodist folding chair   I packed it all in boxes and watched the
CBS Late Movie   The Band Wagon   Fred Astaire dances in a penny
arcade with another man   *Designing Woman*   Lauren Bacall
bit Gregory Peck's ear in a sublime expression of lust   Ingrid
Bergman puts her arm around his shoulders in *Spellbound*   This is
how I would hold a man   Barbra's voice soars   A quarter of a
century later I've got a basement full of bijou and porcelain

Nora Prentiss

Her alabaster cheekbones rise out of the shadows
        as if out of well water,

Ann Sheridan's bedroom eyes slipping
        off the sides of her head,

her shimmering figure moving through dark liqueur,
        pulling us into the inky frame,

making the doctor leave his family
        as effortlessly as she makes us love her.

Baked cement towers above the black enamel streets,
        the Plymouth's slide is a constellation of white dots

in concert against a midnight backdrop. The city's
        grind and shriek, roil and glow

surrounds the coolness of clubs, stale hotel rooms,
        unlighted hallways and offices,

sparking like a transistor panel. Desperate for weeks.
        Be with people. Hear some music.

Open the floral curtains and the dark room dissolves into flames.
        His disfigured face breaks into gray diamonds,

refracted like a kaleidoscope, dazzling as a funhouse mirror,
        the lover in jail, a monster behind a screen.

The Normal Lives of Good People

Her face is the Wrigley Building lit at night,
her eyes billboards, the ponderous

tilt and nod, the reverent. Somewhere, a starlet
lies murdered. A kiss can last an hour, while

her husband's plebeian love crashes over her
in waves of monotone sentiment,

a disembodied voice that haunts her walk
through the impassive. Things must be handled slowly,

touched carefully, the objects larger than our hands,
her son's composition notebook: a Victorian novel,

a nightclub party: the Nuremberg Trials,
while the starlet's blood seeps into the carpet.

One day Chicago will slip into the lake.
When the edifice of her face

sinks to the table, everyone in Arnelo's turns
to watch beauty part her lips.

Lonely, Deeply

My mother's life is my life.
My friend's life is my life.
Here is what the city gives me:

A boyfriend at a bus stop.
Silver towers against an ivory sky.
Granite skin and steel sinews.

The arrangement of mass
follows its own logic,
I in my babushka and bangs

in the cave of the crowded bus,
the kaleidoscope of gray
as we push through revolving doors,

Van Johnson's long eyelashes,
Mama's face eroded by grief,
my arms an afterthought.

The distributor of time
answers to no one.
The war has never ended,

the candles ignite themselves
at St. Patrick's. Lou Gehrig's
trim figure bounds from depth of field

on the left side of the frame.
The lovers' faces are monuments to light
in the brownstones' shadows.

They have faith that gravity won't change,
our bodies won't go flying in the air,
and the music of the spheres is as present

as Franz Waxman's score.
Put a little love in it, Alan King advises.
Today is a day made out of diamonds.

Light and Dark

The city's neon shines on everything,
the factory, the rooms to let, the cavernous dive.

Mirrors on the dancehall girls' top hats
reflect off the men's faces,

the way pain flashes through parts of the body
randomly, and what is flat becomes deep,

a sense of vertigo. This is prewar, inky black
around the frame, cigarette smoke revealed unfurling

like a poltergeist in the sweeping spotlight,
the dancer's placid face filling center frame,

or daylight pooling like phosphorescence
on Maureen O'Hara's hat brim

in the grim canyon of boarding houses,
the castles of Central Park rising

at the end of the street, doors opening and closing:
the pageant in the closet, the hero in the elevator,

the dime in the gutter, the music of rain.
When Tiger Lily White twirls her furs and chiffons

on stage before the black suits, the whole world is ugly.
The flash of the camera bulb at Café Ferdinand

dissects the film into pieces, like amputated limbs.
The city watches out for us, silver skyscrapers

soft at the edges like feathers,
the evening star above the Brooklyn Bridge.

Talent is a stooge for greed.
Dancing means everything to me.

Firmament Shutdown

At 12:01 the governor announced the sky was closed for business.
He led us out of the cave and by a gesture of his hand
indicated the beginning of a night without stars.

Clouds docked at the horizon as quickly as a drop of oil
skids across the surface of a pot of water, the power of inertia.
With a thud the rim of the bowl of heaven landed on the earth beneath.

The storied luminescence of our lakes has gone flat opaque.
And other untold consequences. Mirrors stopped reflecting.
The silhouettes of trees no longer fastened to the skyline.

Shadows moved desultorily, according to their whim,
pooling in the fragrant shallows before rushing to a point,
a planchette on a Ouiji board. Who are we to say they can't procrastinate?

Like us, they have decided time is relative, not absolute.
With no sky pressing on our heads, will our feet disengage from dirt?
We had not heard the sky's revolving thrum until it stopped.

Metaphysical Bailout

"Your father had an accident there: he was put in a pie by Mrs. McGregor."

— Beatrix Potter, *The Tale of Peter Cottontail*

My endeavor is an assemblage of tissue, bone, and nerve
whose code is to lift me up. The engine of music, an enterprise of cells,
a confederacy of one. Even though she's seen it a million times, the projectionist
lets the well-worn movie run itself out. With so many plotlines,
a variable of success is where she could choose to stop it

but doesn't. Wasting away, his winnowed frame left paw prints all over the house
in the Pied Piper's apocalyptic jig toward death. Even then,
he waited until the last minute before opening that door.
Who wouldn't milk the most out of what he's got,
gambling on fate's prerogative to reverse itself?

Scott said, *I choose not to portray my father.*
Sometimes we don't have a choice. We have to go until the going is gone.
Once the gears start moving, all sorts of mystical things happen,
a web of causality. Somewhere is the part that doesn't move.
We are storing it for the future. Bless the active quiet around it,

the value of space surrounding. I will pump ions in the air
with my pink fibrous bellows, a campaign declaiming stasis
but banking on a fall. A child is too young to manage his body,
biting down on pennies, scratching a pox. How the physical can change
in an instant, a head stuck out of a car window on a bridge,

a human finger in a bowl of chili, Nerds and Pepsi. I've made it past
those fears of life-altering fragmentation: unwittingly committing a crime
and going to jail, honestly answering a question that betrays my parents.

Shouldn't it go both ways and the world slip so that what was red is black
and what they all know they now admit?

How I wish to be lovely. Once the frame of reference changes
our signature qualities will emerge from the postdiluvial silt
to shine hallelujah. When the world rights itself, bears will turn into bulls,
mammoths into racehorses, heavy dinosaurs into fine-boned birds.
We'll be seen for who we are, and the past won't matter any more.

The Island of Cats

"He was his island, he was me, he was his cats, he did not exist from the inside out but from the outside in."

—Louise Erdrich, *Love Medicine*

Moses appeared on Washington Avenue
dressed in the tanned and striped skins of cats.
His mother saved him from the plague
by pretending he was already dead.
That's how he became the man outside of time.
He lived on the island of cats,
where he walked backward,
and he wore his clothes backward.
Just as the thief was pulling away in my Honda,
Moses materialized outside my office.
A visitor from the land of apnea,
an arrhythmia of the soul,
he was lonely for story, and came to absorb
our world of golden handshakes, where we believe
if a lie is told often enough
it will magically turn into the truth.
New to traffic jams, the first time
I came to a halt on the freeway,
I thought, the heart has stopped beating,
blood has paused in the arteries.
What Moses doesn't know
is that the old folkways have taken a dive in the polls.
Rather than the coup that's needed,
we've settled for the ritual sacrifice,
but something is dead in the body.
Burning an effigy will not cure an organ failure.
It's just one frustration replaced with another.

With dangerously low levels of iron,
my partner has started eating meat again
before his system shuts down completely.
Sometimes I stop breathing at night, and he prods me awake.
The significance of an episode changes
with its placement in the story, tragic
at the end, comic at the beginning.
When all the planes landed, we could hear the birds.
As the thief sped away in my car,
the television crew set up to interview Moses,
who urged us to pledge allegiance to narratology.
Good evening, zeitgeist. Our top stories tonight . . .

The Island of Cats II

"The greatest wisdom doesn't know itself. The richest plan is not to have one."

—Louise Erdrich, *Love Medicine*

One act of violence changes brain chemistry.
I was never the same boy.

Sometimes the king kills a sacrificial lamb
to prolong his reign.

The dilapidated chassis of the body politic,
an engine of great size and age, unworkable,

forestalls its breakdown with a ritual burning.
Immediately I saw the cats.

Their mouths as fresh and bloody pink as petals.
I am superlative, an offering.

I need to take a break before the brain gets white-hot.
The king has been with cats too long.

Their hearts are like cold balls of silk.
Nothing I could buy or eat would feel so good

as ending this. My cat with a toothache
tries to hide her suffering.

She should say what she means when she means it,
and listen to it later.

People see what enjoys you,
the screen swallowing a face.

After the flying monkeys disemboweled the scarecrow,
the Tin Man said, "Well, that's you all over."

Bang, Bang! Yip, Yip!

I came late to the party of Judy, shy of all the corollaries,
not just the closet, queen, and hag, but the dolls and sketch,
the kitsch und drang. The Bijou at the Student Union, *Easter Parade, The Clock,*
Meet Me in St. Louis, A Star Is Born, The Harvey Girls, Summer Stock,
I put them in the bank, saved them for when I'm old

and gray and settled down, if I ever got the chance
to sneak away from town. Arthur Freed recognized the woman
who had come unstuck in time, Judy Pilgrim. Who's to say
we're born when we should be? The window of the body
is open for only a little while. So he festooned hers

in a Technicolor Victorian habit and set Monument Valley rolling
on a green screen behind. God bless Hollywood, God bless Chimney Rock.
If art lives outside of chronology, why not costume it like a Harlequin?
Her wedding dress is made of clouds. It can't be seen, only imagined,
like the color of the eyes of her fiancé. Most girls coming West

to get married would wear a blue serge suit. God bless organza,
God bless taffeta. She has always wanted to try a Chillicothe sandwich.
We love to honor and oh, baby. Every chorine on Freed's immaculate set
is prettier than Judy, but when the music swells, they all array
their visage toward her. We know life by death.

We are wiser than our actions. When Judy hits her marks, she is
eternal recurrence. We see that *now* is always happening, it never ends.
Pulling her bustle to the side, she glides around the cowboys as if on wheels.
Community becomes architecture. They hoist her on their shoulders
to crown Brueghel's *Tower of Babel.* She views us from the window of a mansion,

sleeps next to our corpse like Faulkner's Emily. So this is the wild West.

Her vibrato trills beyond recognition, the harmony of the spheres.

When her voice goes outside of range, the orchestra changes key to catch up.

When she kicks up her chin with a smile and a sniff, she's won.

Then I'll spend my busman's holiday on the Atchison, Topeka, and the Santa Fe.

Inspiration comes when we don't want it. Navigating
the system's complicated interchanges, an egg-crème moon
balances on a distant viaduct, a right jolly apparition

competing with the skyline's liquid crystal display
stage left. This morning my partner went to work laughing,
You never let me talk, ten years into a projected thirty-year crisis.

How long does midlife last? Thirteen years ago, my Corolla
came to a dead stop on the crowded exit ramp, a marketing director
driving an author to her engagements, when Debra told me

the doctors had found a clot in her brain they knew would kill her,
a time bomb whose detonation no one could predict. I wanted
to do something for this woman I just met, open the channels.

In neutral on the overpass, I couldn't even take an alternate.
Today the acupuncturist said the body is a gift we have
for only so long. *How well will you treat this treasure?*

Tears come at strange times. A million dollar appraisal
on *Antiques Roadshow: With no thought for gain,*
you have collected the things you love. Or the "On the Atchison,

Topeka, and the Santa Fe" sequence in *The Harvey Girls,*
George Sidney's camera pans to Judy emerging from the train.
An ignominious toilet awaits in her future, but on this take she hit her marks.

Or the sixty-one-year-old rampage survivor who, lying on the ground
with the other victims, wrestled the clip from the gunman
before he could reload. On the car radio I hear her testify before Congress:

Changing the past is impossible, no matter how desperately
we want to change it. But it would be a pitiful shame
if no action were taken to change the future.

Debra is still alive, writing in Seattle. Some days you have to roll up
your sleeves and paint a basilica. Until we dissolve into music,
there's just striving and delay, the taste buds changing key.

Tonight I'm slipping through the tangled, irrational freeway with ease.
Spirit writing of the nervous system. *Chi* flows through our feet.
All we have is the body, and someone to lie next to us.

Pretty Poison

Chemicals are a necessary evil.
The assembly line of poison
parades in front of my magnifying glass
whether I am clocked in or not.

The high school majorette
drowns an old man with her thighs,
the way presidents talk with their hands.
She knows where her power lies.
At the end of the river grow monstrous fish.

If I read the newspaper I would become
what I read in the newspaper. The factory
spills pollution like blood into the river.

I saw the authorities before they entered the frame.
Hang a right at the birch trees and cut the lights.
The green points of the forest deliberate like congress.

Now that my head is not filled with worry,
I must remember to leave these days behind.
Monday I slept in the forest in sport coat and tie.

Tuesday came in multiples, refracted
through a row of soda glasses
in the open window of the trailer luncheonette.

All the sharp angles made Wednesday hard to fit on a swing.
Thursday was a red salamander.
Friday loped through twilight on all fours.
Saturday was a bird talking at night.

Sunday started over again nine years ago.
The forests of the northeast
have turned into the beaches of the gulf.
Sometimes you have to be ingenious
just so people will leave you alone.

Rancho Nostalgia II

"My room, bumpkin. I'm pooped."

—Daffy Duck, *The Scarlet Pumpernickel*

So, you're going to put up a fight,
the diner says to her steak.

I wanted something nice,
a girandole, a nocturne,

not a pink necessary chair
or a map of injustices.

A synthetic CEO,
I'll parade down Wall Street

wearing a diadem of wheat,
waving a scepter of corn.

My stock-in-trade is memory,
exchanging shares of *Time* for *Life* magazine.

Nostalgia occurs when affection for some past self
overcomes the will to create a new one.

The mind's enterprise is to erode the surfaces of objects
until they become words.

There is no subsidy program
for the factory of the self.

Just some feelings overlaid by others.
Giving an answer to a previous moment of failure.

What about that moment when the body
was a vessel for the future's operation?

It is still alive. He makes me remember myself
a long time back.

Nostalgia for the past's future. Sure, I'm tired.
We'll take turns resting our heads

on death's pillow. Look at me now, haters,
not commenting on, but living.

Ward Pottery business card holder.
  A gray rabbit looks quizzically
    at the space where name and title should appear.

People I've helped who help me now.
  The gap between train and platform,
    reality and expectation, time is running

oblique. The Victorians believed
  four humors flow through all of us,
    an ocean of bile, islands of flesh.

Dresden was an answer to Coventry. If history
  is a country we can visit, then Hitler, Roosevelt,
    and Churchill are rag dolls in the future's toy box,

trading cards in the same hologram deck. Julian
  of Norwich asked to be bricked in a wall
    in order to get to heaven sooner.

Visitors fed her through a break in the mortar. I believe that evil
  belongs together, Mussolini and the Lockerbie bomber
    sitting at the same lunchroom cafeteria table,

and that everything that survives deserves our love. Salvation
  is on the other side of the world.
    I promise that a detour is a diversion

as surely as I know that we will someday fly outside
  the atmosphere for faster travel. Today
    a team of English scientists discovered

a monster star ten million times brighter than our sun.
Hell falls away the moment when the boaters on the lake
wave to the tourists on the shore.

Finale

A Conversation with My Imaginary Daughter

In a dream I argue with the daughter I never had. In this alternate universe the embodiment
Of a path I didn't choose says she wants to take a cross-country train trip alone,
On the Empire Builder, sweeping through the northern states and Canada.

Fearful of kidnapping, rape, of her getting lost or left behind, or other separations,
I tell her that she cannot go. The problem is, I don't have veto power.
She says the trip is an opportunity for learning,

You know, Mennonites, James J. Hill, flood diversion plans, Buffalo Commons, Emily Carr,
Gang of Seven, Henry Kreisel's *The Betrayal*, Robert Kroetsch's *The Studhorse Man*,
Louis Riel, the Red River Rebellion of 1869, Sharon Butala's *Luna*.

I enter a fugue state. I had thought we'd be close, synergistic in our thinking.
I tell myself I love her—her steady eyes, her straight brown hair casually decorated
With braids—but she's just old enough that I don't entirely know her. My grasp

On our connection is tenuous—I can't read the future, and cause-and-effect escapes me
At my age. Snapping out of it, I come back with arguments as convoluted and fixed as the
Ruching on her embroidered blouse, a hint of peasant flavor.

I've seen this before, an argument at cross purposes, the assembly line production of opinion,
Where the act of manufacture overtakes the product as end result. Repeat this exchange
Too often and Union and Management's talks break down for good.

I know inside that she will go. I'm not helping myself by continuing the argument.
And as Tom Waits asked the beauty of the sky, Wait a minute, can't you see I'm driving?
I acquiesce, although I fear her life growing in a direction I can't attain.

What if the second worst happens? She meets a boy I don't like on the train. She gives up
College dreams to move to his small town in the West. His family owns Main Street.
They have a secure if conservative home, some would say cozy. I don't visit often.

All the old bromides would come back: It was meant to be. What matters is what she wants.
They have a long life ahead of them. They will be happy together. I'll abandon
My dreams for her, her bucking of convention, an unfettered intellect. I'll go back to work.

Before the existence of dialectics, before the invention of opposition, before train cars,
Cubicles, farmhouses, we lived free from the tumors of obstinacy
That grow in our guts, the ones so painful we'd choose no conversation over touching

That pain again. Offices are unnatural environments. When we lived in the wild
We chose what we did, spoke our minds, selected our own beliefs. From the pit of our hearts,
We started each morning by saying to God: Thank you for another day alive.

Closing Credits

The poems in *Rancho Nostalgia* riff on multiple texts, including but not limited to the following films, books, and music, all recommended viewing, reading, and listening:

"Night Song": *Night Song*, 1947, directed by John Cromwell.

"King Arthur and His Mob": *Little Miss Marker,* 1934, directed by Alexander Hall.

"The Eighth Wonder of the World": *King Kong*, 1933, directed by Merian C. Cooper and Ernest B. Schoedsack.

"Sitting by a Fire with You, The Two of Us Planning the Future": *Queen of Outer Space*, 1958, directed by Edward Bernds.

"Quality Street": *Quality Street*, 1937, directed by George Stevens.

"Mr. Purvis": *Too Much Happiness* (Knopf, 2009), Alice Munro, and quotes from the author's 2008 interview with Andrea Walker published on the *New Yorker*'s Web site.

"Murder, My Sweet": *Murder, My Sweet*, 1944, directed by Edward Dmytryk.

"Let's All Chant": "Let's All Chant," 1978, Michael Zager Band, as used in *The Eyes of Laura Mars*, 1978, directed by Irvin Kershner.

"'Til We Meet Again": *Til We Meet Again*, 1940, directed by Edmund Goulding.

"Johnny Guitar": *Johnny Guitar*, 1954, directed by Nicholas Ray.

"Beyond the Rocks": *Beyond the Rocks*, 1921, directed by Sam Wood. The italicized lines are direct quotes of dialogue cards.

"Man Proof": *Man Proof*, 1938, directed by Richard Thorpe.

"The Reality Show": "I Stand Here Ironing," 1961, Tillie Olsen, and *No Name Woman*, 1976, Maxine Hong Kingston.

"The Face Behind the Mask": *The Face Behind the Mask*, 1941, directed by Robert Florey.

"London in the Dark": *Sherlock Holmes and the Secret Weapon*, 1943, directed by Roy William Neill.

"The Adult Season": *The Adult Season*, 2008, BBC.

"Nostalgiarama": *The Spiral Staircase*, 1945, directed by Robert Siodmak. *The Female Man* (Bantam, 1975), Joanna Russ.

"Undercurrent": *Undercurrent*, 1946, directed by Vincente Minnelli.

"Nora Prentiss": *Nora Prentiss*, 1947, directed by Vincent Sherman.

"The Normal Lives of Good People": *The Arnelo Affair*, 1947, directed by Arch Oboler.

"Lonely, Deeply": *Miracle in the Rain*, 1958, directed by Rudolf Maté.

"Light and Dark": *Dance, Girl, Dance*, 1946, directed by Dorothy Arzner.

"The Island of Cats" and "The Island of Cats II": *Love Medicine* (Harper, 1984), Louise Erdrich. The italicized lines in "The Island of Cats II" are direct quotes from *Love Medicine*.

"Bang, Bang! Yip, Yip!" and "Time Bomb": *The Harvey Girls*, 1946, directed by George Sidney.

"Pretty Poison": *Pretty Poison*, 1968, directed by Noel Black.

"Rancho Nostalgia" and "Rancho Nostalgia II": *Rancho Notorious*, 1952, directed by Fritz Lang. The italicized lines in "Rancho Nostalgia II" are direct quotes from "Toward a Prodigal Logic," *First Fire, Then Birds* (Etruscan Press, 2010), H.L. Hix.

"English Poem" is for Éireann Lorsung.

The End

www.ingramcontent.com/pod-product-compliance
Lightning Source LLC
Chambersburg PA
CBHW021508090426
42739CB00007B/526